Contents

The Great Outdoors — Consider playing any or all of these games outdoors! Use rope instead of masking tape to make starting and boundary lines, etc.

Teaching Helps

Course Overview 3
Course Description 4
Decorating Your Center 5
How to Lead the Bible Games Center 6
Supply List 8
Age-Level Characteristics 10
Leading a Child to Christ 13

Bible Games

Session 1—Peace, Be Still
Lesson Overview 14
Bible Story Review Game 15
Bible Verse Game 16

Session 2—Miraculous Meal
Lesson Overview 17
Bible Story Review Game 18
Bible Verse Game 20

Session 3—It Is Written
Lesson Overview 21
Bible Story Review Game 22
Bible Verse Game 24

Session 4—The Good Shepherd
Lesson Overview 25
Bible Story Review Game 26
Bible Verse Game 28

Session 5—Praise in Prison
Lesson Overview 29
Bible Story Review Game 30
Bible Verse Game 31

Reproducible Pages

Peace, Be Still Cards (Session 1) 32
Peace, Be Still Cards for Younger Elementary (Session 1) 33
Peace, Be Still Cards for Older Elementary (Session 1) 34
Eagle Egg Cards (Session 1) 35
Story Answer Cards (Session 2) 36
Beaver Log Cards (Session 2) 37
True or False Cards for Younger Elementary (Session 2) 39
Rock and Roll Cards (Session 3) 40
Rock and Roll Questions (Session 3) 41
Pinecone Cards (Session 3) 42
Dog Bone Cards (Session 4) 43
Wolf Bone Cards for Older Elementary (Session 4) 44
Praise in Prison Cards (Session 5) 45
Praise in Prison Cards for Older Elementary (Session 5) 46
Caribou Cards (Session 5) 47
Caribou Cards for Older Elementary (Session 5) 48

Guidelines for Photocopying Reproducible Pages

Permission to make photocopies of or to reproduce by any other mechanical or electronic means in whole or in part any designated* page, illustration or activity in this book is granted only to the original purchaser and is intended for noncommercial use within a church or other Christian organization. None of the material in this book, not even those pages with permission to photocopy, may be reproduced for any commercial promotion, advertising or sale of a product or service to any other persons, churches or organizations. Sharing of the material in this book with other churches or organizations not owned or controlled by the original purchaser is also prohibited. All rights reserved.

*Do not make any copies from this book unless you adhere strictly to the guidelines found on this page. Pages with the following notation can be legally reproduced:

© 2012 Gospel Light. Permission to photocopy granted to original purchaser only. Climb Higher Bible Games

Gospel Light VBS
Jesus Every Day

Senior Managing Editor, Sheryl Haystead • **Senior Editor,** Mary Gross Davis •
Editors, Janis Halverson, Karen McGraw • **Art Director,** Lori Hamilton Redding

Founder, Dr. Henrietta Mears • **Publisher,** William T. Greig • **Senior Consulting Publisher,** Dr. Elmer L. Towns •
Editorial Director, Biblical and Theological Content, Dr. Gary S. Greig

Scripture quotations are taken from the *Holy Bible, New International Version®*. Copyright © 1973, 1978, 1984
by International Bible Society. Used by permission of Zondervan Publishing House. All rights reserved.

© 2012 Gospel Light, Ventura, CA 93006. All rights reserved. Printed in the U.S.A.

Course Overview

Bible Theme: Philippians 4:19

Daily Promise	Bible Story	Lesson Focus	Bible Verse
Session 1  True PEACE	Peace, Be Still Mark 4:35-41	Jesus gives us peace, no matter what problems we face.	"God is our refuge and strength, an ever-present help in trouble." Psalm 46:1
Session 2  True RICHES	Miraculous Meal Mark 6:30-44; John 6:1-14	Jesus knows what we need and will provide what's best for us.	"My God will meet all your needs according to his glorious riches in Christ Jesus." Philippians 4:19
Session 3  True POWER	It Is Written Matthew 4:1-11	Jesus shows us how to depend on God's powerful Word when we are tempted to sin.	"God is faithful; he will not let you be tempted beyond what you can bear. But when you are tempted, he will also provide a way out." 1 Corinthians 10:13
Session 4  True LOVE	The Good Shepherd Mark 15:1–16:20; John 10:1-18	Jesus loves us so much that He died and rose again so that we can become members of God's family.	"This is how we know what love is: Jesus Christ laid down his life for us." 1 John 3:16
Session 5  True HOPE	Praise in Prison Acts 16:16-40	Jesus is with us, so we can be fearless about our future.	"We wait in hope for the Lord; he is our help and our shield. In him our hearts rejoice, for we trust in his holy name." Psalm 33:20-21

Teaching Helps • 3

Course Description

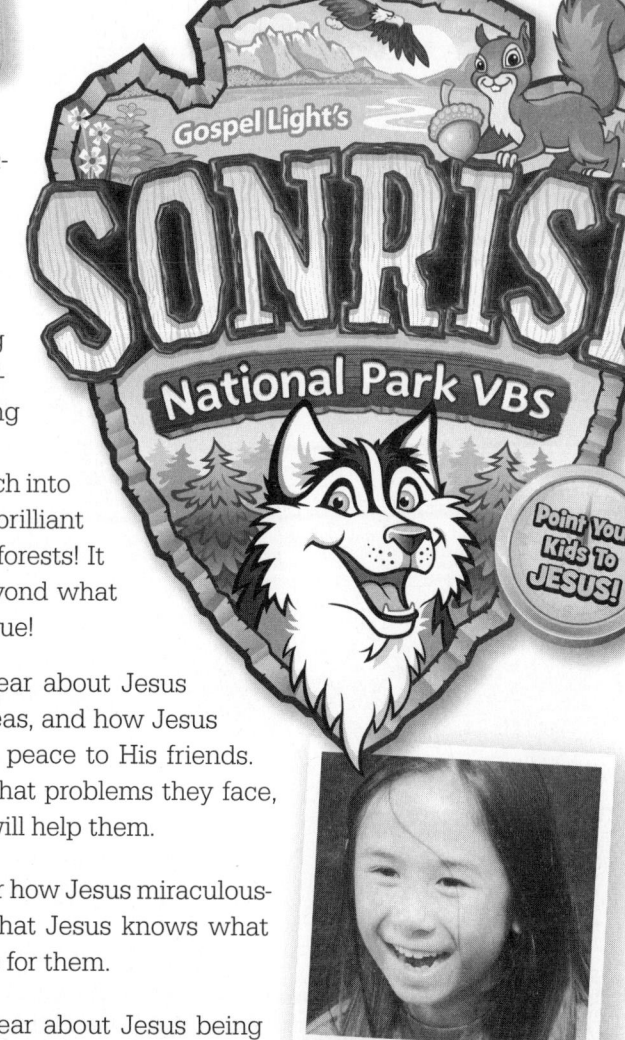

Discover the best destination of the summer—*SonRise National Park*! Come to a land of invigorating power and beauty where there is nothing between you and God's big sky! Kids will enjoy the thrills of daily treks where they can face extreme challenges and learn to depend on the promises of Jesus—promises each of us can cling to. They will discover the true treasure described in Philippians 4:19, "My God will meet all your needs according to his glorious riches in Christ Jesus."

With easy-to-find decorations, you can turn your church into a wilderness adventure park with rugged mountains, brilliant wildflowers, glassy glaciers, amazing animals and deep forests! It is here that your kids will discover that they can go beyond what they think they know to discover what is essential and true!

▶ **True Peace** In Session 1, kids will hear about Jesus and His friends in a boat on stormy seas, and how Jesus was able to calm the storm and give peace to His friends. Children will realize that no matter what problems they face, Jesus is loving and powerful and He will help them.

▶ **True Riches** In Session 2, kids will hear how Jesus miraculously fed over 5,000 people and realize that Jesus knows what kids need and will provide what's best for them.

▶ **True Power** In Session 3, kids will hear about Jesus being tempted by Satan, and will discover that Jesus shows them how to depend on the power of God's Word when they are tempted to sin.

▶ **True Love** In Session 4, kids will hear about Jesus the Good Shepherd. They will learn that Jesus loves each one of them so much that He died and rose again so that they could become members of God's family.

▶ **True Hope** In Session 5, kids will learn that even when they can't see Him, Jesus is with them just like He was with Paul and Silas in prison. Kids can be fearless about the future because Jesus is always with them and has a plan for them.

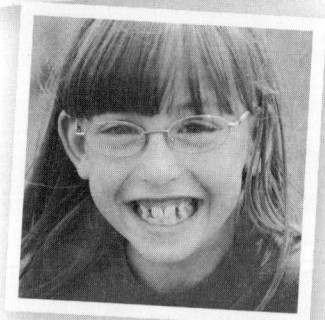

This summer, take your children to *SonRise National Park* and get them started on a life-changing journey that will last the rest of their lives. Children will know that no matter what extreme challenges may come their way in life, they will have the indescribable, all-powerful, unchangeable, unwavering Jesus to guide their way.

Decorating Your Center

Glacier Bay

Create a cool, clear bay formed from a melting glacier. On the rocky shore, kids play Bible games in the great outdoors. For additional information and fun ideas check out myvbsparty.com and the Gospel Light VBS Facebook page.

Level 1

➤ Use these easy decorating supplies, available from Gospel Light. Attach **Decorating Posters**, **Bible Teaching Posters** and **Wall Cutouts** to the walls. Add color with **balloons** and **pennants**.

Level 2

➤ Place an **artificial pine tree** in a corner of the room. Perch a **stuffed bald eagle**, or other **stuffed bird** on top of tree.

➤ Set a **stuffed squirrel** near the tree, with a pile of **unshelled nuts**.

➤ Set a **small inflatable boat** or **kayak** in a corner of the room. Add a **fishing pole**, **tackle box** and **fisherman's vest** or **life vest**.

Level 3

➤ Paint **Glacier Bay Backdrop** (available in *National Park Decór & More*) and attach to wall.

➤ Crumple **iridescent**, **light blue**, **or clear cellophane** and glue to the ice portion of the mural to make three-dimensional glacial ice.

➤ Trace back and front of **Seaplane Pattern** (available in *National Park Decór & More*), paint, glue to **heavy cardboard or foam core** and cut out. Hang plane from the ceiling, or set it on the ground near the glacier.

Teaching Helps ● 5

How to Lead the Bible Games Center

Play and learn! The Bible Games Center is often kids' favorite VBS center. Rarely are children aware of the direct learning value of a game, but they participate enthusiastically because they enjoy the game. The following games provide plenty of teamwork and fun, while helping children memorize and review the session's Bible verse or review the Bible story as well as apply these Bible truths to everyday life.

Remember, the goal is for everyone to have fun while learning, not to produce winners and losers. Before beginning each game, briefly discuss with your group the purpose of the game and the attitudes that help everyone to have fun.

Bible Games Center Basics

Either by yourself or with another leader or helper complete the following steps:

1. Together with your VBS Director, determine whether you will use this center for Bible Story Review Games, Bible Verse Games, or a combination of the two.
2. Familiarize yourself with each day's lesson overview. Read the Bible story references, Bible Story Recap and Bible Verse so that you can easily talk about them with the children. Memorize the Lesson Focus and Daily Promise so that you can guide conversation with your children toward these learning objectives.
3. For each session, review the Goals for Each Child. These aims are primarily met in the Bible Story Center. One or more of these learning objectives will be met by each Bible game. (Note: Only the Grades 3 and 4 goals have been included in this guide. Grades 1 and 2 and Grades 5 and 6 goals differ slightly.)
4. Read the game chosen for each session and decide how you will adapt it for each age level you will teach. These games are appropriate for third- and fourth-grade skill levels. However, adaptations are provided to simplify each game for use with first and second graders or to make it more challenging for fifth and sixth graders. Use the adaptations appropriate to the skill level of each class.
5. Collect supplies or submit a list to your VBS Director or Supply Coordinator. Group general supplies together and supplies specific to each day in a labeled box or bag. Prepare items as needed.
6. Shortly before VBS, decorate your assigned classroom (see p. 5).
7. Lead children in the game as directed. Use the conversation suggestions provided with each game. These questions are designed to help children understand the Bible truths and discover how those truths apply to their everyday lives. In the game discussion, be alert for natural openings to talk with children about the wonderful opportunity they have to receive God's love and forgiveness and to become members of His family. See "Leading a Child to Christ" on page 13 for more information.

> **Note:** The games in this book are written for children in Grades 3 and 4. Adaptation ideas for children in Grades 1 and 2 and Grades 5 and 6 are also included. Look for age-appropriate sets of Bible story review questions that have been provided as needed. Please use the suggested adaptations and questions (or use your own) to keep games, questions and conversation age-appropriate.

Tips for Leading Games

- **Offer a practice round.** When playing a game for the first time with your class, play it a few times just for practice. Players will learn the rules best by actually playing the game.
- **The Great Outdoors** Consider playing some or all of the games outside!
- **Vary the process by which teams are formed.** Randomly divide children into teams. Play the game once. Then announce that the person on each team who is wearing the most red (or blue, or is the tallest or has the longest hair, etc.) should rotate to the team to his or her right. Then play the game again. As you repeat this rotation process, vary the method of rotation so that children play with several different teammates each time.
- **If children are rotating through various activity centers,** remember that some classes may not have heard the Bible story before coming to your center. If this is the case, you may choose to play the Bible Verse Game instead of the Bible Story Review Game. Other options would be to play the previous day's game as a review or to briefly tell the session's Bible story (or read aloud the Bible Story Recap) before playing the game.

Memory Verse Contests

As a feature of their VBS programs, many churches hold Memory Verse contests. But because individual memorization contests often discourage children for whom memorization is difficult, we recommend instead having contests in which each class works together to earn points all week long! For each session of VBS, create a new point goal with prizes for each team. Members of each team earn points toward their team's point goal through Bible verse memorization, attendance, bringing a Bible or friend, etc. Make each point goal achievable by the next session. For example, if by the second session, 25 points have been earned, a prize will be given to the team members. At each closing assembly, announce which teams achieved—or surpassed—their point goal.

Make the theme come alive for your VBS students and they will be even more enthusiastic about joining in the activities! As leaders of the Bible Games Center, give yourselves a new name inspired by adventure in a northern wilderness: Pinecone Pete, Floatplane Fran, Salmon Sal, etc. Wear theme-related clothing, such as ranger-style clothing, climbing gear, fishermen's vests and hiking boots. Decorate your room as described on page 5 and play the SonRise songs. You'll have as much fun as the kids—maybe more!

Teaching Helps • 7

Supply List

Use this handy list as you gather all the supplies you will need to teach the Bible Games Center for five sessions.

General Supplies

- [ ] Bibles
- [ ] Sessions 1-5 Bible Story Posters from *Bible Teaching Poster Pack*
- [ ] Sessions 1-5 Bible Verse Posters from *Bible Teaching Poster Pack*
- [ ] *Music & More* CD and player
- [ ] markers
- [ ] scissors or paper cutter
- [ ] masking tape

Session 1

Capsize the Cups
- [ ] Peace, Be Still Cards (p. 32)

For each team of 6 to 8—
- [ ] 8 paper or plastic cups, a different color for each team

For each student—
- [ ] uninflated balloon

Eagle Egg Hunt
- [ ] Eagle Egg Cards (p. 35)

For each team of 6 to 8—
- [ ] 12 plastic eggs, one color for each team
- [ ] empty egg carton

Session 2

Fill the Basket!
- [ ] Story Answer Cards (p. 36)

For each team of 6 to 8—
- [ ] small basket or box

Beaver Logs
- [ ] Beaver Log Cards (pp. 37-38)
- [ ] tan paper

8 • Teaching Helps

Session 3

Rock and Roll Race
- Rock and Roll Cards (p. 40)
- Rock and Roll Questions (p. 41)

For each team of 6 to 8—
- empty 2-liter bottle

Pinecone Pickup
- Pinecone Cards (p. 42)

For each team of 6 to 8—
- different color of paper

Session 4

Silly Sheep and Shepherds

For each team of 5—
- 5 white balloons
- 5 coins
- hula hoop

Husky Races
- Dog Bone Cards (p. 43)

For each team of 6 to 8—
- different color of paper
- bath or beach towel
- bowl

Session 5

Chain Reaction
- Praise in Prison Cards (p. 45)

For every team of 6 to 8—
- different color of paper

Snow Scrape
- Caribou Cards (p. 47)
- cotton balls
- drinking straws

For every team of 6 to 8—
- different color of paper

Teaching Helps • 9

Age-Level Characteristics

Grades 1 and 2

Physical
The term "perpetual motion" may be used to describe children this age. Small-muscle coordination is still developing and improving. Girls are often ahead of boys at this stage of development.

Teaching Tip: Adjust skills needed for games to accommodate children's different physical abilities. For example, allow younger children to stand closer to a throwing target.

Social
Children are concerned with pleasing their leaders. Each child is also struggling to become socially acceptable to his or her peer group. The Golden Rule is a tough concept at this age. Being first and winning are very important. Taking turns is hard, but this skill improves by the end of the second grade. A child's social process moves gradually from *I* to *you* and *we*.

Teaching Tips: Playing games provides opportunities for children to practice taking turns. Help each child accept the opinions and wishes of others and consider the welfare of the group as well as his or her own welfare. Call attention to times when the group cooperated successfully and thank them.

Spiritual
Children can sense the greatness, wonder and love of God when helped with visual and specific examples. The nonphysical nature of God is baffling, but God's presence in every area of life is generally accepted when parents and teachers communicate this belief by their attitudes and actions. Children can think of Jesus as a friend, but they need specific examples of how Jesus expresses love and care. This understanding leads many children to belief and acceptance of Jesus as their personal Savior. Children can comprehend talking to God anywhere, anytime and in their own words, and children need regular opportunities to pray.

Teaching Tip: The gospel becomes real as children feel love from those who talk about God. Show your faith in a consistent, loving way to model the loving nature of God to children. As you play games with children, look for natural opportunities to talk with them about God's love for them and His desire for them to become members of His family.

Emotional

Children are experiencing new and frequently intense feelings as they grow in independence. Sometimes the child finds it hard to control his or her behavior. There is still a deep need for approval from adults and a growing need for approval by peers.

Teaching Tips: Seek opportunities to help each child in your group KNOW you love him or her. Show genuine interest in each child and his or her activities and accomplishments. Learn children's names and use them often, especially when you have something positive to say!

Cognitive
There is an intense eagerness to learn, and children of this age ask lots of questions. They like to repeat stories and activities. The concept of time is limited. Thinking is here and now, rather than past or future. Listening and speaking skills are developing rapidly; girls are often ahead of boys. Each child thinks everyone shares his or her view. Children see parts, rather than how the parts make up the whole and think very literally.

Teaching Tip: Talk simply and clearly, avoiding words the child may not understand. Use teams of mixed genders so that boys don't dominate physically or girls dominate academically.

10 • Teaching Helps

Age-Level Characteristics

Grades 3 and 4

Physical
Children at this level have good large- and small-muscle coordination. The girls are generally ahead of the boys. Children can work diligently for longer periods but can become impatient with delays or their own imperfect abilities.

Teaching Tip: When playing games that involve taking turns, keep teams small so that kids don't wait long to have a turn.

Social
Children's desire for status within the peer group becomes more intense. Most children remain shy with strangers and exhibit strong preferences for being with a few close friends. Some children still lack essential social skills needed to make and retain friendships.

Teaching Tip: Look for the child who needs a friend. Move near that child and include him or her in what you are doing. If he or she needs a partner to play the game, be that partner!

Spiritual
Children are open to sensing the need for God's continuous help and guidance. They can recognize the need for a personal Savior. There may be a desire to become a member of God's family. Children who indicate an awareness of sin and a concern about accepting Jesus as Savior need careful guidance without pressure.

Teaching Tips: Give children opportunities to pray. Talk about the forgiving nature of God. Talk personally with a child who shows interest in trusting the Lord Jesus. Use the *God Loves You!* booklet (available from Gospel Light) to explain how to join God's family.

Emotional
This is the age of teasing, nicknames, criticism and using increased verbal skills to vent anger. By eight years of age, children have developed a sense of fair play and a value system of right and wrong. At nine years of age, children are searching for identity beyond membership in the family unit.

Teaching Tips: You have a great opportunity to be a Christian example at a time when children are eagerly searching for models! Encourage children's creativity and boost their view of themselves. Let children know by your words and by your actions that "love is spoken here" and that you will not let others hurt them or let them hurt others.

Cognitive
Children are beginning to realize there may be valid opinions besides their own. They are becoming able to evaluate alternatives and are less likely than before to fasten onto one viewpoint as the only one possible. Children are also beginning to think in terms of "the whole." Children think more conceptually and have a high level of creativity. By this stage, however, many children have become self-conscious as their understanding has grown to exceed their abilities in some areas.

Teaching Tips: As you play Bible Verse games, ask questions to help children understand the meaning of the words. To check understanding, invite children to say the verse in their own words.

Teaching Helps • 11

Age-Level Characteristics

Grades 5 and 6

Physical

Children have mastered most basic physical skills, are active and curious, and seek a variety of new experiences. Rapid growth can cause some preteens to tire more easily.

Teaching Tip: Be sure to have both male and female teen helpers who participate enthusiastically in the games. Seeing older kids enjoying the games will encourage preteens who otherwise might worry about being "too cool" to play the games.

Social

Friendships and activities with their peers flourish. Children draw together and away from adults in the desire for independence. The child wants to be a part of a same-gender group and usually does not want to stand alone in competition.

Teaching Tip: When you play games that require scorekeeping, move on to the next round or activity without announcing the score or winner. If the activity is fun and compelling, most kids will never notice the omission.

Spiritual

Children can have deep feelings of love for God, can share the good news of Jesus with a friend and are capable of involvement in outreach and service projects. The child may seek guidance from God to make everyday and long-range decisions.

Teaching Tips: Provide opportunities for children to make choices and decisions based on biblical concepts. Encourage children to use these concepts as they play games together.

Emotional

Children are usually cooperative, easygoing, content, friendly and agreeable. Be aware that some preteens experience unsteady emotions and can quickly shift from one mood to another.

Teaching Tips: Be patient with changes of feelings. Give many opportunities to make choices with only a few necessary limits. Take time to listen as children share their experiences and problems with you.

Cognitive

Children of this age are verbal! Making ethical decisions becomes a challenging task. They are able to express ideas and feelings in a creative way. By 11 years of age, most children have begun to be able to reason abstractly. They begin to think of themselves as grown up and at the same time question adult concepts. Hero worship is strong.

Teaching Tips: Include lots of opportunities for talking, questioning and discussing in a safe, accepting environment. Ask children for their ideas of how the games could be played better.

12 ● Teaching Helps

Leading a Child to Christ

One of the greatest privileges of serving in VBS is helping children become members of God's family. Pray for the children you teach and ask God to prepare them to understand and receive the good news about Jesus. Ask God to give you the sensitivity and wisdom you need to communicate effectively and to be aware of opportunities that occur naturally.

Because children are easily influenced to follow the group, be cautious about asking for group decisions. Offer opportunities to talk and pray individually with any child who expresses interest in becoming a member of God's family—but without pressure. A good way to guard against coercing a child to respond is to simply ask, "Would you like to hear more about this now or at another time?"

When talking about salvation with children, use words and phrases they understand; never assume they understand a concept just because they can repeat certain words. Avoid symbolic terms ("born again," "ask Jesus to come into your heart," "open your heart," etc.) that will confuse these literal-minded thinkers. (You may also use the evangelism booklet *God Loves You!* which is available from Gospel Light.)

1. God wants you to become His child. Why do you think He wants you in His family? (See 1 John 3:1.)

2. You and I and every person in the world have done wrong things. The Bible word for doing wrong is "sin." What do you think should happen to us when we sin? (See Romans 6:23.)

3. God loves you so much that He sent His Son to die on the cross to take the punishment for your sin. Because Jesus never sinned, He is the only One who can take the punishment for your sin. On the third day after Jesus died, God brought Him back to life. (See 1 Corinthians 15:3-4; 1 John 4:14.)

4. Are you sorry for your sin? Tell God that you are. Do you believe Jesus died for your sin and then rose again? Tell Him that, too. If you tell God you are sorry for your sin and believe that Jesus died to take your sin away, God forgives you. (See 1 John 1:9.)

5. The Bible says that when you believe that Jesus is God's Son and that He is alive today, you receive God's gift of eternal life. This gift makes you a child of God. This means God is with you now and forever. (See John 1:12; 3:16.)

There is great value in encouraging a child to think and pray about what you have said before responding. Encourage the child who makes a decision to become a Christian to tell his or her parents. Give your pastor and the child's Sunday School teacher(s) his or her name. A child's initial response to Jesus is just the beginning of a lifelong process of growing in the faith, so children who make decisions need to be followed up to help them grow. The discipling booklet *Following Jesus* (available from Gospel Light) is an effective tool to use.

Teaching Helps • 13

Peace, Be Still

Bible Story

Mark 4:35-41

Bible Verse

God is our refuge and strength, an ever-present help in trouble. Psalm 46:1

Lesson Focus

Jesus gives us peace, no matter what problems we face.

Goals for Each Child

1. DISCOVER that when the disciples were afraid in the storm, Jesus responded to their call for help and rescued them;
2. DESCRIBE what it means to say that Jesus gives us peace;
3. ASK Jesus for help and peace for a situation in my life;
4. CHOOSE to rely on the peace Jesus offers by becoming a member of God's family, as the Holy Spirit leads.

Bible Story Recap

Jesus and His disciples were traveling across the Sea of Galilee when a sudden furious storm began. Jesus was sleeping in the boat while the disciples frantically worked at trying to stay afloat. In a panic, a disciple came to Jesus and asked Him, "Don't You care if we drown?"

Jesus showed that He not only cared for them but also that He had complete power over nature. He spoke; the wind stopped—and the storm was over! In the peace after the storm, the stunned disciples asked each other, "Who is this? Even the wind and waves obey Him!" They were amazed by Jesus' power that had so quickly brought peace! Jesus provides that same peace to all who choose to follow Him.

Heart Prep

Welcome to SonRise National Park VBS! Sometimes the first day of VBS can feel out of control—almost like a big storm is brewing. Kids are getting used to the schedule, leaders are figuring out their responsibilities and everyone is trying to get to know each other. Everyone can have a case of the jitters! But have no fear! Jesus offers True Peace in the midst of ALL types of storms—even the first day of VBS.

Today's Bible story reminds us that even though the disciples panicked during a terrible storm, Jesus never panicked! He calmed the storm with His voice. Wow! In this story we not only see the power of Jesus, but also that because of His power, we can trust Him, the Son of God, to give us True Peace in the middle of whatever situation comes our way. It may not always turn out the way we want or expect, but we can trust that He is in control.

What is worrying you today? Tell Jesus about it—and don't worry! He isn't sleeping. He is ready to show His power in whatever storm you feel brewing. Ask Him to open your eyes to see how He is at work. Ask Him to pour His peace into you and through you so that you can share it with the children and other volunteers at VBS today and all week. And don't forget to be thankful, even in the storms. That's when we get to see Jesus up close!

Daily Recap

At the end of each lesson, take time to reflect on what happened. Use these questions as a guide:

- What worked well today? Did you experience any first-day "storms"?
- As you prepare for Session 2, ask God to give you His peace in the midst of a busy VBS schedule.
- Read aloud the name of each child in your group. Pray for each one, inviting God to help that child understand His love and salvation this week.

If children are rotating through various activity centers, remember that some classes may not have heard the Bible story before coming to your center. If this is the case, you may choose to play the Bible Verse Game instead of the Bible Story Review Game. Or you may play the previous session's game for review, briefly tell the Bible story or read the Bible Story Recap aloud before playing the game.

Bible Story Review Game
(20-25 minutes)

Capsize the Cups

Materials

- [ ] Bible
- [ ] Session 1 Bible Story Poster from *Bible Teaching Poster Pack*
- [ ] Peace, Be Still Cards (p. 32)
- [ ] scissors or paper cutter
- [ ] masking tape

For each team of 6 to 8—

- [ ] 8 paper or plastic cups, a different color for each team

For each student—

- [ ] uninflated balloon

Preparation:

- [ ] Display Bible story poster.
- [ ] For each team of six to eight players, copy one set of Peace, Be Still Cards.
- [ ] Cut cards apart and shuffle each team's cards separately.
- [ ] For each team, place each card from the team's set inside a separate cup.
- [ ] Place each team's set of cups in a line on a separate table.
- [ ] Use masking tape to make a starting line approximately 10 feet (3 m) away from tables.

Procedure:

1. Players form teams of six to eight. Teams line up behind starting line. Give each player a balloon.
2. At your signal, first player in each team runs to team's cups and then inflates his or her balloon.
3. Player releases air from balloon, trying to capsize only one cup. When cup has been knocked over, player removes card from cup. If more than one cup is capsized, player must re-set cup(s).
4. Player takes card, returns to tag next player and goes to the end of the line.
5. When all the team's cups have been knocked over and cards recovered, team works together to put cards in story order. The first team to finish reads cards aloud in order. Play again as time and interest allow.

Wrap It Up:

Sometimes severe weather can be very frightening and cause a lot of damage. There are times in all of our lives when things going on around us may feel just as scary as a big storm. Today's story reminds us how Jesus proved He has power over the weather—and He has power over whatever problems we face in our lives, too! Show Session 1 Bible Story Poster.

➤ **What problems did the disciples face?** (A lot of wind. Big waves. Boat filling with water. Boat might capsize. Fear they would drown.)

➤ **How did Jesus take care of all of these problems?** (Told the wind and waves to stop—and they did!)

➤ **What problems might make a kid your age ask for Jesus' help?** (Being scared of the dark. Parents arguing. Being bullied. Sister lying.)

➤ **How does remembering what Jesus did give us true peace?** (If Jesus can stop a huge storm, He also cares for us when we have problems. Jesus is powerful and will use His power to help us.)

What is our Daily Promise today? Pause for children to respond, "True Peace!" **No matter what problems we face, we can remember that Jesus loves us. He is powerful and He will help us!**

Younger Elementary Adaptation: Instead of using Peace, Be Still Cards on page 32, use Peace, Be Still Cards for Younger Elementary on page 33. As children put cards in story order, discuss with them the part of the story shown in each picture.

Older Elementary Adaptation: Instead of using Peace, Be Still Cards on page 32, use Peace, Be Still Cards for Older Elementary on page 34. Students first find Scripture references and read them aloud, and then write a brief caption on the back of each card before putting the cards in story order.

Session 1 • Grades 1 to 6 • 15

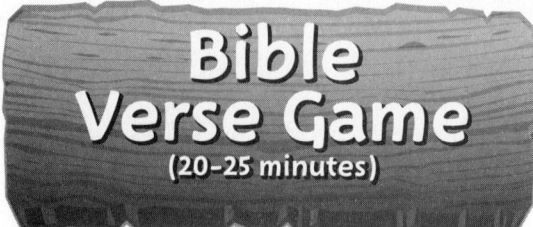

Bible Verse Game
(20-25 minutes)

Eagle Egg Hunt

Materials
- [ ] Bible
- [ ] Session 1 Bible Verse Poster from *Bible Teaching Poster Pack*
- [ ] Eagle Egg Cards (p. 35)
- [ ] scissors or paper cutter

For each team of 6 to 8—
- [ ] 12 plastic eggs, one color for each team
- [ ] empty egg carton

Preparation:
- [ ] Display Bible verse poster.
- [ ] For each team, copy a set of Eagle Egg Cards. Cut cards apart; place each team's cards in its set of plastic eggs, one card per egg.
- [ ] Hide eggs all around the playing area.

Procedure:
What is our Daily Animal today? Pause for volunteers to respond, "Eagle." **Let's go on an Eagle Egg Hunt!**

1. Players form teams of six to eight. Give each team an egg carton and assign each team a different color of egg to find.
2. At your signal, players hunt for eggs in their team's color. As eggs are found, they are placed in team's egg carton.
3. When a team finds all its eggs, team members race to open eggs, remove cards and put cards in Bible verse order.
4. To show that they are finished, team members flap their arms like wings and shriek like eagles.
5. The first team finished reads the verse aloud from the verse cards. Repeat as time and interest allow.

Wrap It Up:
What is our Daily Promise? Pause for volunteers to respond, "True Peace!" **Eagles remind us that Jesus can give us True Peace. God made eagles to sense when a storm is coming. An eagle will fly to a high spot and wait for the storm. When the storm comes, the eagle peacefully and safely rides the winds above the storm.** Show Session 1 Bible Verse Poster. **Even in the hard times and storms of life, Jesus helps us to be like the eagle and "fly above" the trouble when we ask for His help.**

➤ **What are some other words for "refuge"?** (A shelter, a hideout, a protected place.)
➤ **What does this verse tell us about God?** (He is our refuge—a safe place. He is our strength—He makes us strong. He is ever-present—always with us. He helps us when we're in trouble.)
➤ **How can knowing these things about God give us True Peace?** (God promises to give us protection and strength when we need it. We don't have to worry. We can talk to God any time. We can trust Him to care for us.)
➤ **Describe a situation when a kid your age would need to depend on God's True Peace.** (Parent loses job. Moving to new home. School is hard. Someone you love has cancer.)

God loves us; He wants all of us to know the power of His Son, Jesus. When we join God's family, we can ask Jesus for His help and power anytime. We can experience God's True Peace forever!

Younger Elementary Adaptation: Number the backs of the cards in verse order to help kids place them correctly.

Older Elementary Adaptation: Replace half the verse cards with blank index cards. Older children print the missing words on the blank cards before putting cards in order.

16 ● Session 1 ● Grades 1 to 6

Miraculous Meal

TRUE RICHES

Bible Story

Mark 6:30-44; John 6:1-14

Bible Verse

My God will meet all your needs according to his glorious riches in Christ Jesus. Philippians 4:19

Lesson Focus

Jesus knows what we need and will provide what's best for us.

Goals for Each Child

1. DISCOVER that Jesus provided for the physical and spiritual needs of a crowd of people;
2. DESCRIBE the true riches Jesus gives to meet our needs;
3. THANK Jesus for providing for me and ask His help in sharing generously with others;
4. CHOOSE to have true riches by trusting Jesus to provide for me and becoming a member of God's family, as the Holy Spirit leads.

Bible Story Recap

Sailing to a quiet spot across the Sea of Galilee, Jesus and His disciples planned to get some rest. But crowds of people followed them on foot! Jesus had compassion on the people. He taught them many things and then asked the disciples to feed the people.

The disciples were shocked! How could they ever afford to feed so many people? But of course, Jesus had a plan. Andrew found and brought to Jesus a boy who had a lunch of two small fish and five small loaves of bread. Jesus thanked God for the food, broke it into pieces and began giving it to the disciples to deliver to the hungry crowd.

The food kept coming until over 5,000 men plus women and children all ate their fill. The disciples were amazed. The people were satisfied. Thousands of men, women and children experienced how Jesus gave God's True Riches. Jesus promises True Riches to us, too.

Heart Prep

Have you ever been grocery shopping and gotten everything you thought you needed, only to come home and realize you forgot the very thing you needed most? Many people go through life thinking they can work hard and meet all their needs. Their bank accounts are full, their families are intact and their careers are flourishing. Yet they are constantly pursuing a need they are not quite sure how to fill—the need for a relationship with God.

In today's Bible story we will discover that Jesus had compassion on a large group of people. He saw both their physical and spiritual needs as they gathered; they were hungry for more than food for their stomachs. Jesus met the needs of this enormous crowd. He first met their spiritual needs as He spoke to them of God's love. Then He nourished their physical bodies in a miraculous way! Some of the people realized that Jesus offers the True Riches that would satisfy their deepest need—to know Him.

As you lead children today, the needs may be obvious to you: more help, paper, glue, snacks, time, etc. But what are the real needs of each child? They may need a listening ear, a tender touch, a genuine smile, a laugh at a goofy joke or an encouraging word—and especially, the good news of Jesus' love for them. Ask God to help you pour out the riches of His love and acceptance on the children today. May the true needs of the children be met by His True Riches through you, His true follower.

Daily Recap

At the end of each lesson, take time to reflect on what happened. Use these questions as a guide:

- What was your greatest need today? What did you do about it? How did Jesus meet that need?
- Thank God for meeting that need and ask for the strength to lead the kids during Session 3.
- Be prepared to tell about a time when knowing a particular Bible verse helped you to obey God.

Grades 1 to 6 • Session 2

Bible Story Review Game
(20–25 minutes)

Fill the Basket!

Materials
- Bible
- Session 2 Bible Story Poster from *Bible Teaching Poster Pack*
- Story Answer Cards (p. 32)
- scissors or paper cutter
- masking tape

For each team of 6 to 8—
- small basket or box

Preparation:
- Display Bible story poster.
- For each team, photocopy and cut apart one set of Story Answer Cards.
- Use masking tape to make a starting line on one side of the playing area.
- Mix up each set of cards and place each team's set of cards at the opposite side of the playing area. Station a leader or helper beside each pile of cards.

Procedure:
In today's story, Jesus miraculously provided food for over 5000 people. Show Session 2 Bible Story Poster. **There was so much food that Jesus told His disciples to gather up the leftovers—and they gathered 12 baskets full! Let's use our baskets to gather the right answers! Learning God's Word helps us understand the True Riches that Jesus offers us.**

1. Players form teams of six to eight. Teams line up behind the starting line. Give the first player in each line a basket.
2. Read aloud a Bible Story Review Question (see p. 19). After question is read, first player on each team passes basket back over his or her head to the next player, who then passes it back between his or her legs; players pass basket in over-and-under fashion to reach last player in line.
3. The last player runs with basket to team's pile of Story Answer Cards, finds the correct answer and then shows it to team leader or helper. If the answer is correct, player drops card into basket and runs back to the front of team's line. If player picks up an incorrect answer card, player must return card to pile, find correct answer card and show it to leader before proceeding.
4. When the first player on each team has collected the correct card, read the next question. Play continues until all of the questions have been answered. Repeat as time and interest allow.

Wrap It Up:
Just like Jesus provided what the people truly needed when He miraculously fed them, He will also give us what we truly need! What's our Daily Promise? Pause for volunteers to answer, "True Riches!" **We can trust that Jesus knows what we need. He will give us what is best for us—True Riches!**

Younger Elementary Adaptation: Photocopy and cut out a set of True or False Cards for Younger Elementary (p. 39). Place cards in a basket and hand them to a helper to hold. During game, helper with basket stands about 10 feet (3 m) from the teams. The first team to pass basket all the way down the line runs to leader and chooses a card from the basket. Helper reads sentence aloud and team answers. If the answer is False, the team explains why the answer is false. Repeat as time and interest allow.

Older Elementary Adaptation: The first team finished with a round chooses a motion for the next round: Pass basket only overhead, turn around in a circle and then pass the basket, clap three times and then pass it, hop on one foot while passing the basket, etc.

After every two or three rounds, ask one of the Older Elementary Questions (p. 19), to promote discussion and deeper thinking among older students.

18 • Session 2 • Grades 1 to 6

Bible Story Review Questions

- **Why did Jesus and His disciples go in a boat to the far side of the Sea of Galilee?** (They wanted to rest.)
- **How many people had come to hear Jesus teach?** (Over 5,000.)
- **Why did so many people want to meet Jesus?** (He healed sick people. He taught them the truth about God.)
- **Why did the disciples look for food?** (Jesus told them to because the people were hungry.)
- **What was in the boy's lunch?** (Five loaves of bread and two fish.)
- **Before feeding the people, what did Jesus do?** (Gave thanks to God and broke bread and fish into pieces.)
- **How many people ate until they were full?** (All of them!)
- **How many baskets of food were left over?** (There were twelve baskets.)

Younger Elementary Questions

- **More than 5,000 people came to hear Jesus teach. True or false?** (True.)
- **Jesus told the people about God. True or false?** (True.)
- **Jesus told the disciples to give the people food. True or false?** (True.)
- **The disciples went to the market to buy food. True or false?** (False. There were no markets around to buy food from.)
- **Nobody offered to share their food. True or false?** (False. A boy offered to share his food.)
- **The boy's lunch was five sandwiches and two apples. True or false?** (False. The boy's lunch was five small loaves of bread and two fish.)
- **Before feeding all the people, Jesus gave thanks to God. True or false?** (True.)
- **There was no food left over. True or false?** (False. There were 12 baskets of food left over.)

Older Elementary Questions

- **When you think about the way Jesus provided food for so many people, what does that tell you about Jesus' ability to provide for us? What are some of the needs a kid your age may have that Jesus can help him or her with?** (Parents argue. Scared of bully.)

- **People usually think of riches as having a lot of money, nice cars, lots of toys and video games, fancy clothes and other things. But True Riches are what Jesus gives us in order to live the life God has planned for us. What are some of the True Riches Jesus gives us?** (People who love us, peace, God's Word, salvation.)
- **When you read in Philippians 4:19 how God provides for us from His glorious riches in Jesus, how does that make you feel about Jesus? How does it make you feel to know that He will help you when you will need help in the future?** (Peaceful. Thankful. Glad.)
- **Imagine you've been having trouble on your soccer team. You don't seem to be playing as well as usual and you're not getting along with all of your teammates. What are some True Riches you can ask for from Jesus to help you in this situation?** (Courage to do your best. Patience to get along with others.)

Grades 1 to 6 ● Session 2 ● 19

Bible Verse Game
(20-25 minutes)

Beaver Logs

Materials
- [ ] Bible
- [ ] Session 2 Bible Verse Poster from *Bible Teaching Poster Pack*
- [ ] Beaver Log Cards (p. 37-38)
- [ ] tan paper
- [ ] scissors or paper cutter
- [ ] masking tape

Preparation:
- [ ] Display Bible verse poster.
- [ ] For each team of four to six players, photocopy a set of Beaver Log Cards onto tan paper. (Be sure to make two-sided copies that back up correctly.) Cut apart cards.
- [ ] Place a set of each team's "logs" in a separate section of the playing area, with all of the pictures face-up.
- [ ] Use masking tape to make a starting line approximately 10 feet (3 m) from the log cards.

Procedure:
What is today's animal? Pause for volunteers to respond, "Beavers." **Beavers remind us that God provides for all our needs. They work hard to give their animal families what they need and collect logs in order to build their dams. In our game today, we're going to collect logs, too—or at least, log CARDS!**

1. Children divide into teams of four to six. Teams line up behind starting line.
2. On your signal, the first player on each team runs to the log pile, selects a log, examines picture and decides whether or not the picture shows True Riches. If player decides picture does NOT show True Riches, he or she chooses another card.
3. If player thinks a card shows True Riches, he or she turns the card over. If the card shows words from the Bible verse, player takes card, returns to team, tags the next player and goes to the end of the line. If the card reads, "Try again!" player returns card to the pile, chooses another card and then decides whether or not that card shows True Riches.
4. Play continues until a team has collected eight log cards. Then team puts cards in Bible verse order. First team finished says the verse aloud.

Wrap It Up:
Point to Session 2 Bible Verse Poster. **The word "glorious" means "wonderful" or "amazing." As members of God's family, we know that Jesus will take care of us and meet our needs.**

▸ **What are some needs kids your age have?** (Food. Water. Clothes. A place to live. People who care for us. To learn.)
▸ **What are some things kids your age want?** (Toys. Cool electronics. Lots of friends. To get good grades. Be good at sports.)
▸ **What are God's glorious riches?** (His love. Forgiveness for our sins. Peace. Being part of God's family. Answers to prayer.)
▸ **How are God's riches different from things others might say are riches?** (God's riches are things that only God can give us.)

What is our Daily Promise? Pause for volunteers to answer, "True Riches!" **When we don't get what we want or something we think we deserve or need, we can remember that Jesus has the best plan. We can trust Jesus to understand what we need. He will provide what is best for us!**

Younger Elementary Adaptation: Number cards in verse order on the "verse words" side. Have a leader or helper near card piles to help children read the words on the cards.

Older Elementary Adaptation: Specify a way for children to move as they retrieve the cards: heel-to-toe, backwards, hopping on one foot, etc.

It Is Written

Bible Story

Matthew 4:1-11

Bible Verse

God is faithful; he will not let you be tempted beyond what you can bear. But when you are tempted, he will also provide a way out." 1 Corinthians 10:13

Lesson Focus

Jesus shows us how to depend on God's powerful Word when we are tempted to sin.

Goals for Each Child

1. DISCOVER that when Jesus was tempted to sin, He showed the power of God's Word, the Bible;
2. PLAN actions that help us follow Jesus' example when we feel tempted to sin;
3. THANK Jesus for promising to help me when I am tempted to sin;
4. CHOOSE to have true power by believing God's Word and becoming a member of God's family, as the Holy Spirit leads.

Bible Story Recap

Jesus spent 40 days in the desert, praying and spending time alone with God His Father. At the end of that time, Satan tried to tempt Jesus to turn desert stones into bread. Jesus rejected Satan's temptation and used God's Word to answer: "'Man shall not live on bread alone, but on every word that comes from the mouth of God" (Matthew 4:4).

Next, Satan took Jesus to the top of the Temple and tried to talk Him into jumping off so that God's angels would rescue Him. Jesus said, "It is also written: 'Do not put the Lord your God to the test'" (Matthew 4:7). Finally, Satan offered Jesus all the kingdoms of the world—IF Jesus would bow and worship Satan. But Jesus said, "Away from me, Satan! For it is written: 'Worship the Lord your God, and serve him only'" (Matthew 4:10). Knowing and using God's Word gave Jesus True Power to overcome Satan's temptations. And that same power is available to us!

Heart Prep

My dad was a carpenter, and it seemed like when he had his tool belt on he could fix or build anything. Today's lesson shows us how God's Word is like our spiritual tool belt. In this story from the early days of Jesus' ministry, we see Jesus at His weakest physically, being tempted in all the ways we are tempted. Yet Jesus had the tool He needed to defeat the attacks of His enemy. That tool is God's Word. Jesus was so familiar with God's Word that when Satan tried to use it against Him, Jesus wasn't fooled. God's Word is where we learn what True Power is. God's Word is our true "power tool" both for resisting the enemy and for leading kids at VBS. And the power of God's Word is what kids need as they grow up in this world with many temptations trying to lure them away from following Jesus.

As you study the Bible story and the Bible verse today, ask God to remind you of the True Power of His Word when you face various temptations. Ask God to help you depend on His power to share the way out of temptation with the boys and girls at VBS today.

Daily Recap

At the end of each lesson, take time to reflect on what happened. Use these questions as a guide:

➤ Did the kids take away their need to know and memorize God's Word?

➤ Which child had difficulty getting along with others or making friends? Plan to befriend him or her to help meet their needs.

➤ For Session 4, be prepared to share briefly and appropriately how you came to rely on Jesus as your Good Shepherd.

Bible Story Review Game
(20-25 minutes)

Rock and Roll Race

Materials
- [ ] Bible
- [ ] Session 3 Bible Story Poster from *Bible Teaching Poster Pack*
- [ ] Rock and Roll Cards (p. 40)
- [ ] Rock and Roll Questions (p. 41)
- [ ] scissors or paper cutter

For each team of 6 to 8—
- [ ] empty 2-liter bottle

Preparation:
- [ ] Display Bible story poster.
- [ ] Photocopy and cut out a set of Rock and Roll Cards for each team. For each team, make a photocopy of Rock and Roll Questions.
- [ ] For each team, place Rock and Roll Cards facedown in a circle about 10 feet (3 m) in diameter. Place a 2-liter bottle on its side to use as a spinner.
- [ ] Station a helper near each team and hand him or her a copy of the Rock and Roll Questions.

Tip: Instead of photocopying the Rock and Roll Cards, print the instructions found on the cards on the flat sides of fist-sized rocks.

Procedure:
A compass helps us point ourselves in the direction we should go. We're going to spin the bottles like compass pointers. Then we'll follow the directions we find.

1. Players form teams of six to eight.
2. Each player takes a turn to spin the bottle. Player turns over the card the bottle points to and reads the instructions on the card.
3. Team follows the instruction on card.
4. Leader reads aloud a Bible Story Review question. Player who read rock card answers question or chooses a volunteer from the team to answer.
5. As soon as question is answered, player spins the bottle to show who will have the next turn. Play continues until all the questions are answered or as time and interest allow.

Wrap It Up:
Show Session 3 Bible Story Poster. **Today we saw how Jesus used God's Word to stop the devil and obey God. He showed us what True Power is.**

➤ **What are some ways you can get to know and understand God's Word?** (Read the Bible. Listen to Bible teachers. Listen to songs based on Bible verses. Talk with a parent about the Bible. Memorize Bible verses. Say Bible verses as prayers to God.)

➤ **What makes it hard to learn God's Word?** (Forgetting to read the Bible. Not paying attention to what it says.)

➤ **What are some ways a kid your age might be tempted?** (To copy someone else's answers on a test. To cheat in a game. To lie to avoid getting in trouble.)

What's our Daily Promise? Pause for kids to respond, "True Power!" **There are a lot of people and things in this world that are very powerful. But we get True Power from God's Word. In today's Bible story, Jesus showed us how to depend on God's powerful Word when we are tempted to sin. Knowing God's Word gives us True Power to say "no" to temptation and obey God instead!**

Younger Elementary Adaptation: Leaders ask Younger Elementary Questions. If the answer is false, ask children to explain why the answer is false.

Older Elementary Adaptation: In addition to Bible Story Review Questions, add Older Elementary Questions to promote discussion.

22 • Session 3 • Grades 1 to 6

Bible Story Review Questions

- How many days was Jesus in the desert? (Forty.)
- What did Jesus do in the desert? (Fasted. Prayed.)
- Why did Satan try to get Jesus to do something wrong? (Satan didn't want Jesus to follow God's plan. Satan didn't want Jesus to be able to take the punishment for our sins.)
- What did Satan tempt Jesus to do with rocks? (Turn rocks into bread.)
- What did Satan tempt Jesus to do at the Temple? (Jump off a high place so that angels would have to save Him.)
- What did Satan say He would give Jesus if Jesus would worship him? (All the kingdoms of the world.)
- What did Jesus do every time Satan tempted Him to do wrong? (Said "No." Repeated God's Word back to Satan.)
- What could you do when you are tempted to do something wrong? (Remember what God's Word says. Say what God's Word says! Pray, asking God for help. Say "No.")

Younger Elementary Questions

- Jesus was in the desert for 12 days. True or False? (False. Jesus was in the desert for 40 days.)
- While in the desert, Jesus ate three good meals a day. True or False? (False. While in the desert, Jesus didn't eat any food.)
- Satan visited Jesus in the desert. True or False? (True.)
- Satan tempted Jesus to turn rocks into fish. True or False? (False. Satan tempted Jesus to turn rocks into bread.)
- Satan said shepherds would protect Jesus if He jumped off the roof of the Temple. True or False? (False. Satan said angels would protect Jesus if He jumped off the roof of the Temple.)
- Satan said he would give all the kingdoms in the world to Jesus if Jesus would worship him. True or False? (True.)
- Knowing God's Word helped Jesus when Satan tempted Him. True or False? (True.)
- When someone tempts us to do wrong, we should call them names. True or False? (False. We should remember God's Word. We can ask God to help.)

Older Elementary Questions

- Imagine you have been alone in the desert for 40 days without anything to eat. How would you be feeling? If you were faced with the same three temptations as Jesus, which be the hardest to say "No" to? Why?
- What are some common temptations kids your age face? What are some things kids can do to help them say "No" to temptation?
- How could you say the words of 1 Corinthians 10:13 as a prayer when you are tempted to do something wrong?
- One day after VBS, your mom takes you and a friend on some errands. While you're in the grocery store and your mom is busy at the checkout, your friend steals a candy bar and tells you to take one, too. What do you do?

Grades 1 to 6 • Session 3 • 23

Bible Verse Game
(20-25 minutes)

Pinecone Pickup

Materials

- [ ] Bible
- [ ] Session 3 Bible Verse Poster from *Bible Teaching Poster Pack*
- [ ] Pinecone Cards (p. 42)
- [ ] scissors or paper cutter
- [ ] masking tape

For each team of 6 to 8—
- [ ] different color of paper

Preparation:

- [ ] Display Bible verse poster.
- [ ] For each team, on a different color of paper, photocopy Pinecone Cards and cut apart. Shuffle all the cards together and attach cards in random order to one or more walls in playing area (or on the ground if played outside).
- [ ] Use masking tape to make a starting line approximately 10 feet (3 m) from area where Pinecone Cards are placed.

Procedure:

Red squirrels run from place to place, gathering pinecones and nuts. They store their food in a *cache* (KASH) to eat during the long, cold winter. Today we're going to act like squirrels and run from place to place to tag and say the words of our verse!

1. Players form teams of six to eight. Assign a color of card to each team. Teams line up behind starting line.
2. On your signal, the first player on each team runs to the walls covered with Pinecone Cards, trying to find the card in team's color that has the first words to the verse. The player places a hand on the card to tag it, reads the words aloud, and then searches for the next verse card.
3. Player continues until he or she has tagged and read aloud all the verse cards in team's color. Player then returns to team and tags next player.
4. Team members may help the player by repeating the verse loudly or directing player to the correct Pinecone Cards. Play continues until all the teams have completed the challenge.

Wrap It Up:

God made red squirrels to store up pinecones and nuts so they'll have food when they are hungry. When we read God's Word, we are like the squirrels. We're storing up what we need so that when faced temptation, we have the True Power of God's Word to help us say "No" and obey God instead!

➤ **Who or what do you depend on every day?** (Parents. Friends. Teachers. Mom's car to start. Lights, computer and TV to go on.)

➤ **What are some ways kids your age are tempted?** (To cheat in school. To do what parents told you not to do. To hide a mistake, like breaking a window. To make excuses for not doing right.)

➤ **God says He will always provide a way out. That means He will always help us find a way to say "No" to temptation. What can help us find God's way out?** (Learn God's Word. Ask God to show you. Pray for wisdom. Ask a trusted teacher for advice.)

Jesus shows us how to depend on God's powerful Word when we are tempted to sin. So keep on storing Bible verses by reading and memorizing God's Word. Then you'll have the power to help you say "No" when you are tempted!

Younger Elementary Adaptation: Number the Pinecone Cards in verse order on the front sides.

Older Elementary Adaptation: Older children move to cards according to directions called out by the leader: heel-to-toe, backwards, tiptoe, hopping on one foot, etc.

The Good Shepherd

Bible Story

Mark 15:1—16:20; John 10:1-18

Bible Verse

This is how we know what love is: Jesus Christ laid down his life for us. 1 John 3:16

Lesson Focus

Jesus loves us so much that He died and rose again so that we can become members of God's family.

Goals for Each Child

1. DISCOVER that Jesus' death and resurrection show His great love;
2. DESCRIBE who Jesus is and why He is the Good Shepherd;
3. DESCRIBE why I need Jesus to be my shepherd;
4. CHOOSE to receive Jesus' true love and become a member of God's family, as the Holy Spirit leads.

Bible Story Recap

As the time came near for Jesus to finish the work God had sent Him to do, Jesus told about a good shepherd. This shepherd was not like a hired hand: He knew the sheep by name; the sheep knew his voice and would follow him. Then Jesus said that He is the Good Shepherd, we are His sheep and that the Good Shepherd would willingly lay down His life for His sheep.

Many people were glad to listen to Jesus but the religious leaders were afraid of Him because so many loved and followed Him. They paid to have Jesus betrayed. Jesus was arrested, tried and beaten. Jesus went willingly, for He had already said He would lay down His life for His sheep. When Jesus was taken to the Romans to be nailed to a cross, Jesus willingly laid down His life to take the punishment for our sin. But that wasn't the end! On the third day, Jesus rose from death to show us that He is stronger than anything. We have nothing to fear—we can be forgiven and join God's family forever!

Heart Prep

Every day at SonRise National Park VBS there is an opportunity to share what it means to become a member of God's family. But today is the day to clearly explain that God sent His Son, Jesus, to be our Savior. The greatest act of love known to man was Jesus' laying down His life for us. First John 3:16 tells us, "This is how we know what love is: Jesus Christ laid down his life for us."

Jesus gave us a beautiful picture of what His True Love looks like: a good shepherd who cares for his sheep. A good shepherd knows each sheep by name. He provides good pasture for the sheep. He protects the sheep from wolves. A good shepherd will give up his life to keep his sheep safe. Jesus' disciples didn't understand what Jesus was talking about when He compared Himself to a good shepherd. But because hindsight is much clearer than foresight, we can see that when Jesus died on the cross, He demonstrated His love for us. We are unable to pay the price for our sins, so the Good Shepherd paid that price. The best part is that He not only laid down His life for us, but because of His authority over death, He also took His life up again! The living Jesus gives eternal life to those who turn from their sin and put their faith in Him.

Pray that Jesus will give the kids at SonRise National Park VBS an understanding of their need for the True Love that only comes from following the Good Shepherd!

Daily Recap

At the end of each lesson, take time to reflect on what happened. Use these questions as a guide:

- What worked well today? Pray for the energy to finish VBS strong.
- Think back to today's session: Which children seemed most interested in talking about joining God's family? Which ones seemed to still have questions? Ask God to give you the opportunity and the words to talk further with these children.
- As you prepare for the final session of VBS, pray for each child by name. Ask God to water the seeds that were planted today; this may have been the first time some were told what Jesus did for them!

Grades 1 to 6 • Session 4 • 25

Bible Story Review Game
(20-25 minutes)

Silly Sheep and Shepherds

Materials

- [ ] Bible
- [ ] Session 4 Bible Story Poster A and Poster B from *Bible Teaching Poster Pack*
- [ ] *Music & More* CD and player

For each team of 5—
- [ ] 5 white balloons
- [ ] 5 coins
- [ ] hula hoop

Preparation:

- [ ] Display Bible story posters.
- [ ] Place a coin inside each balloon and then inflate balloons. Tie balloons and scatter them around the playing area.
- [ ] Lay hula hoops several feet away from each other in the center of the playing area.

Tip: The weight of the coins in the balloons will not only keep them from going too far while players tap them, but also will make balloons move unpredictably, which adds to the fun!

Procedure:

Jesus told about the ways a good shepherd cares for sheep. Let's play a game where we are shepherds and these balloons are our sheep!

1. Players form teams of five and stand beside the team's hoop. The hoops serve as each team's sheep pen.
2. Play "This Is How We Know" from CD. As music plays, each player takes a turn to run to a balloon sheep and gently tap it to guide it into the team's sheep pen. Players may not pick up balloon sheep.
3. Play continues until a team has five balloon sheep in the sheep pen. When a team has five balloon sheep inside, all team members are called to sit down around the sheep pen. Stop the music; teams freeze.
4. Leaders read aloud a Bible Story Review Question for the seated team to answer.
5. Scatter the balloon sheep back into the playing area and restart music. Play continues until all review questions have been asked or as time permits.

Wrap It Up:

In today's story, Jesus calls Himself the Good Shepherd. Show Session 4 Bible Story Posters. **Jesus said that as the Good Shepherd, He would lay down His life for His sheep. He did that by dying on the cross. That's how Jesus showed True Love for us—He laid down His life.**

▶ **What do people have to do to join God's family?** (Ask God to forgive their sins. Believe Jesus took the punishment for their sins. Ask God to help them obey Him. Ask Jesus to make them part of God's family.)

▶ **What would you tell a kid your age it means to join God's family?** (You are God's child, part of God's family. It means you'll live in heaven forever. It means Jesus loves you and will forgive your sin when you ask Him.)

▶ **What might keep a kid your age from joining God's family?** (Doesn't know about it. Scared of what people might say. Not sure what it means.)

- **If you are part of God's family, what would you say is the best thing about it?** (Knowing I am forgiven. Knowing I will go to heaven. Knowing Jesus is with me and will help me.)

What's our Daily Promise? Pause for kids to respond, "True Love!" **Jesus showed True Love for us by willingly dying on a cross. But the good news is, Jesus didn't stay dead! Jesus came back to life and lives today. Jesus was willing to do this so that we can join God's family. He wants each of you to join God's family and live with Him in heaven forever!**

Younger Elementary Adaptation: Instead of asking Bible Story Review Questions, ask Younger Elementary Questions below. If the answer is false, team explains why it is false.

Older Elementary Adaptation: For each team, on separate balloons, print one word of the sentence "Jesus is the Good Shepherd." Then put all balloons in a central area, placing hula hoops at the edge of playing area. Each team must gather "sheep" so that each hula hoop sheep pen contains one of each word from the sentence. Teams hold balloon sheep in order to complete the sentence before sitting down around sheep pen.

Bible Story Review Questions

- **What kind of shepherd did Jesus say He is?** (Good.)
- **What are ways a good shepherd cares for His sheep?** (Provides what they need—food, water, shelter. Knows them. Protects them. Lays down his life if necessary.)
- **What did Jesus say about a hired shepherd?** (Sheep don't know his voice or follow him. He doesn't protect sheep. He runs from danger.)
- **What did Jesus say about Himself as the Good Shepherd?** (He willingly lays down His life for His sheep.)
- **Why did some people tell lies about Jesus to get Him arrested?** (They didn't like the things Jesus was telling people. They were afraid the people would love and listen to Jesus instead of them.)
- **What happened to Jesus after He was arrested?** (He was beaten. He was killed on a cross.)
- **What happened three days after Jesus was killed?** (He rose from the tomb. Jesus was alive again.)
- **What does it mean for us today that Jesus died on the cross and lives again?** (We can become members of God's family. As members of God's family, we can live with Him forever in heaven. We can be forgiven of our sins.)

Younger Elementary Questions

- **Jesus said that a good shepherd forgets his sheep. True or False?** (False. A good shepherd knows his sheep and cares for them.)
- **A good shepherd knows the sheep and cares for them. True or False?** (True.)
- **Sheep are very smart and don't need a shepherd. True or False?** (False. Sheep need a shepherd.)
- **A good shepherd runs away from a wolf. True or False?** (False. A good shepherd protects his sheep from a wolf.)
- **Jesus said, "I am the Good Shepherd. I lay down My life for My sheep." True or False?** (True.)
- **A good shepherd is willing to die to protect or save the sheep. True or False?** (True.)
- **Jesus said He was going to come back to life—and He did. True or False?** (True.)
- **Because Jesus died on the cross and came back to life again, we can become members of God's family. True or False?** (True.)

Older Elementary Questions

- **How does 1 John 3:16 describe God's love? How did Jesus lay down His life? How can we "lay down our lives" to show love to others?**
- **Since Jesus was willing to do so much to show love to us, what can we do in return to show love to Him? To show others we love Him?**
- **How can you show the kind of love described in 1 John 3:16 to a person who feels lonely? A sick person? A person who needs to know about Jesus? A person who is here today at VBS?**
- **You and your friends are trying to decide which DVD to rent. One friend's parents won't let her watch R-rated movies, so your friends want to watch a movie without her. What do you think? What will you do? How can you show love to ALL your friends?**

Grades 1 to 6 • Session 4

Bible Verse Game
(20-25 minutes)

Husky Races

Materials
- [ ] Bible
- [ ] Session 4 Bible Verse Poster from *Bible Teaching Poster Pack*
- [ ] Dog Bone Cards (p. 43)
- [ ] scissors or paper cutter
- [ ] masking tape

For each team of 6 to 8—
- [ ] different color of paper
- [ ] bath or beach towel
- [ ] bowl

Optional–
- [ ] Bonz® Dog Bone candy or other candy prize for all teams

Preparation:
- [ ] Display Bible verse poster.
- [ ] For each team, photocopy a set of Dog Bone Cards onto a different color of paper. Cut cards apart.
- [ ] Mix up all colors of cards together. Place 10 cards in each "dog bowl" at one end of the playing area.
- [ ] Use masking tape to make a starting line approximately 10 feet (3 m) from bowls.

Procedure:
Huskies LOVE to get doggie treats! You all are huskies and there are bowls full of doggie treats for each team—but you can only have your own team's color of doggie treat! It's a race to get your team's doggie treats and then put them in verse order!

1. Players form teams of six to eight. Assign a Dog Bone Card color to each team and give each team a towel.
2. Teams pair up: a smaller player acts as the musher and a larger player acts as the husky. The musher sits on the towel and the husky pulls the musher to the bowls. The musher gets off, finds a Dog Bone Card in the team's color and then gets back onto towel. (Note: If students cannot be pulled on towels, set a stuffed dog on each towel. Student pulls the dog to the bowls. If dog falls off, student must replace dog before moving.)
3. Husky pulls musher back to the line and then the next pair takes a turn.
4. Play continues until each team retrieves all verse cards in their team's color. Each team then works together to put cards in verse order. The first team to do so reads the verse aloud. Play another round as time and interest allow. (Optional: Give players Bonz Dog Bone candy or other candy prize.)

Wrap It Up:
What is our Daily Promise? Pause for volunteers to respond, "True Love!" God made huskies to love people. They are very friendly and need the attention and care of their owners. The husky reminds us that God made us to need Him! God sent Jesus so that we can know how much God loves us.

➤ **What did Jesus do to show true love to us?** (He laid down His life. Died on the cross.)

➤ **How is Jesus' death different from the deaths of other people who die?** (Jesus died willingly. Jesus' death was part of God's plan to rescue us. Jesus died to take the punishment for our sin. Jesus didn't stay dead. He came back to life and is alive forever.)

➤ **Why did Jesus lay down His life for us?** (Jesus loves us. He wants us to live with Him in heaven forever. He died so that we could have our sins forgiven, join God's family and have eternal life.)

We use the word "love" often: We say, "I love pizza." "I love this game." "I love the Dodgers." But today's verse tells us what True Love is. We know Jesus' love is true because He didn't just say it, He demonstrated it. Jesus loves us so much that He died on the cross to take the punishment we should have gotten for our sins. He rose again to prove that we don't need to be afraid of death. He has made the way for us to join God's family!

Younger Elementary Adaptation: Number the backs of cards in verse order.

Older Elementary Adaptation: Copy a set of Wolf Bone Cards (page 44) in each team's color. Mix these in with the Dog Bone Cards. As teams put verse cards in order, they will have to determine which cards have correct words and which do not.

Praise in Prison

Bible Story

Acts 16:16-40

Bible Verse

We wait in hope for the Lord; he is our help and our shield. In him our hearts rejoice, for we trust in his holy name. Psalm 33:20-21

Lesson Focus

Jesus is with us, so we can be fearless about our future.

Goals for Each Child

1. DISCOVER that Paul and Silas praised Jesus even in prison, because they trusted Jesus and had hope in Him;
2. DESCRIBE situations in which kids my age might be worried or feeling hopeless;
3. ASK Jesus to help me trust Him so that I can have hope and confidence in every situation;
4. CHOOSE to have true hope, follow Jesus every day and become a member of God's family, as the Holy Spirit leads.

Bible Story Recap

As God's family grew, Paul and Silas traveled to share the good news about Jesus. When a slave girl followed them for days, Paul commanded the spirit to leave the girl, in Jesus' name—and it did! But this evil spirit was the also source of the girl's fortune-telling ability. Her owners had Paul and Silas arrested, beaten and thrown in jail.

In the pitch-black prison, Paul and Silas knew that Jesus was with them. They prayed and sang praises to God—everyone in the jail could hear them! God caused a huge earthquake that opened all the prison doors and broke the chains. The jailer thought the prisoners had escaped, so he was about to take his own life when Paul stopped him. The jailer asked, "What must I do to be saved?" Paul and Silas gladly replied, "Believe on the Lord Jesus Christ!" The jailer took them to tell his entire household the good news about Jesus and they all joined God's family!

Paul and Silas were able to praise God from their prison cell because of the hope they had in Jesus. Everyone who chooses to follow Jesus can have that same hope.

Heart Prep

Have you ever felt anxious about the future? Maybe after college graduation you wondered if you would be able to make it on your own. I know that after I gave birth to my first child, I panicked. *How will I ever take care of this tiny person?* I had no idea what I was doing! The future felt like a dark, foggy tunnel. How do you think the kids in your group feel about their future? Some may not have given tomorrow a second thought, while others might be worried about where they will live next month.

Regardless of what our future holds, we know that we can have hope because God is in control. Paul and Silas had this True Hope and as a result they were able to sing in that pitch-black prison after being beaten nearly to death. They didn't know if they would live or die the next day—and they probably had pretty bad headaches, backaches and any number of other aches! Yet they chose to face their pain in praise. It was a concert that literally brought the house down! Through their pain and their praise, others came to a saving knowledge of Jesus Christ.

We want our kids to know that no matter what situation they face today or in the future, they can have True Hope by trusting in Jesus. He promises to be with us always. He provides fellow believers to walk with us along the journey. Jesus is in control of our future and when we put our hope in Him, we will see Him glorified just like Paul and Silas did. I know I want a front-row seat at that concert, don't you?

Daily Recap

At the end of each lesson, take time to reflect on what happened. Use these questions as a guide:

➤ What was the best thing you think the kids learned this week? What was the best thing you learned this week?
➤ Thank God for the things that happened this week—the best, the worst and the most laughable! Ask Him to help you plan ways to stay in contact with the kids you taught.
➤ Ask the Holy Spirit to help you and your children understand and hold on to True Hope in Jesus.

Grades 1 to 6 ● Session 5 ● 29

Bible Story Review Game
(20–25 minutes)

Chain Reaction

Materials
- [ ] Bible
- [ ] Session 5 Bible Story Poster from *Bible Teaching Poster Pack*
- [ ] Praise in Prison Cards (p. 45)
- [ ] scissors or paper cutter
- [ ] marker
- [ ] masking tape

For each team of 6 to 8—
- [ ] different color of paper

Preparation:
- [ ] Display Bible story poster.
- [ ] Photocopy a set of Praise in Prison Cards onto a different color of paper for each team. Cut cards apart; shuffle all cards together place in a large heap at one end of the playing area.
- [ ] Use masking tape to make a starting line approximately 10 feet (3 m) from cards.

Procedure:
Paul and Silas were thrown into a dark prison. When it is dark we have to use our sense of touch. In our game, we'll have to use our sense of touch to know when it's time for a turn.

1. Designate a color of card for each team. Players form teams of six to eight and line up, laying their hands on the shoulders of the person ahead of them. Players keep eyes closed.

2. When teams are ready, leader quietly taps the last player on each team's line to start. Player gently taps shoulders of the person in front of him or her, who then taps the next player in line, causing a chain reaction all the way to the front of the line.

3. When the player at the front of the line is tapped, he or she opens eyes, runs to cards and takes a card in the team color. Player then returns to the rear of the line, places card on floor, taps the shoulders of the person ahead of him or her and begins the chain reaction again.

4. Play continues until all the cards are picked up. Each team then works together to put the cards in story order. First team to finish reads cards in the correct order. Repeat as time and interest allow.

Wrap It Up:
Show Session 5 Bible Story Poster. **Paul and Silas praised God and did what was right when it seemed like things were turning out wrong. Even when we might be afraid or worried about what might happen, God tells us to do the right thing—and then trust Him to care for us and help us. That gives us hope for the future, no matter what!**

➤ **What did Paul and Silas do for the slave girl?** (In Jesus' name, they told the evil spirit to leave her and it did.)

➤ **What happened to Paul and Silas after the evil spirit left the girl?** (The owners got mad. They could not make money from the slave girl's fortune telling. They had Paul and Silas arrested, beaten and put in jail.)

➤ **How did Paul and Silas show that they believed Jesus was with them, even though they could not see Him?** (They prayed, sang and praised God in prison.)

➤ **How did God respond to Paul and Silas' praise and prayer?** (He caused an earthquake. He freed them. He helped them share the good news of Jesus with the jailer and his family.)

It is hard to imagine being brave in what looked like a hopeless situation. But Paul and Silas showed that they had hope. The word "hope" means to trust confidently, expecting good. **What is our Daily Promise?** Pause for volunteers to reply, "True Hope!" **When we're part of God's family, we can have True Hope! Even though we can't see Jesus, He is with us in every situation.**

Younger Elementary Adaptation: Number the backs of the Praise in Prison Cards in story order.

Older Elementary Adaptation: Instead of Praise in Prison Cards, use Praise in Prison Cards for Older Elementary (p. 46) players. Players look up and read the Bible references, and then write words in the empty conversation balloons.

> **Note:** For a physical challenge, tell players to keep arms outstretched above the shoulders of the player ahead during the game—it's harder than it sounds!

Bible Verse Game
(20-25 minutes)

Snow Scrape

Materials

- [ ] Bible
- [ ] Session 5 Bible Verse Poster from *Bible Teaching Poster Pack*
- [ ] Caribou Cards (p. 47)
- [ ] scissors or paper cutter
- [ ] cotton balls
- [ ] drinking straws
- [ ] masking tape

For each team of 6 to 8—
- [ ] different color of paper

Preparation:

- [ ] Display Bible verse poster.
- [ ] For each team, photocopy a set of Caribou Cards on a different color of paper; cut cards apart.
- [ ] Mix all colors of team cards together; place cards in a row along the finish line. Place cotton balls over the cards, so that some cotton balls cover each card, but the color of the card is still visible.
- [ ] Use masking tape to make starting and finish lines approximately 10 feet (3 m) apart from each other.

Procedure:

Our daily animal today is the Caribou. Caribou is a Native American word that means "snow scraper." During the winter, caribou move the snow to get to their food. We are going to move some "snow," too—so that we can pick up the words of the Bible verse. All we need is a little help from drinking straws!

1. Children form teams of six to eight and line up behind starting line. Helpers give each team member a straw. Players place straws behind their ears until they reach the finish line. Designate the color of card for each team's "food."

2. At your signal, first player from each team crawls to the finish line, finds a card in the team's color, and then uses his or her straw to blow off each cotton ball that covers only that card. When card is uncovered, player takes that card in hand, crawls back to team and tags the next player.

3. Play continues until all cards for the team are collected. Teams then put the cards in verse order. First team to correctly order the verse cards reads the verse aloud. (For an extra challenge, players move cards into Bible verse order using only straws—no hands!)

Wrap It Up:

We know that if we belong to God's family, Jesus is with us all of the time. Even though we can't see Him, we can remember that Jesus is our help and shield. That makes us rejoice in Him! We can have True Hope for the future, because we know that Jesus loves and cares for us.

➤ **According to our verse, who is it we can wait in hope for?** (The Lord. Jesus.)

➤ **What are some times kids your age might feel like there is no hope?** (When parents argue. When family members are hurt or sick. When we see scary things on TV that have happened.)

➤ **What would you say to another kid who feels hopeless?** (Jesus gives me hope. God cares about you. Let's pray together about this. How can I help you?)

What is our Daily Promise? Pause for children to respond, "True Hope!" **Caribou find hope and safety by sticking together in a herd, even in hard times. When we're part of God's family, Jesus wants us to remember that He is always with us. But He wants us to stay close to Him and to each other. Knowing we have Jesus and have each other gives us what?** Pause for volunteers to answer, "True Hope!"

Younger Elementary Adaptation: Number backs of the cards in verse order. Scatter fewer cotton balls.

Older Elementary Adaptation: Photocopy Caribou Cards for Older Elementary on page 48, as well as the Caribou Cards on page 47. The first team to put the words in verse order chooses a situation from the other cards and answers as a team. Then, they choose another team to choose a situation and respond to it. Teams continue choosing other teams until all the situation cards have been answered.

Grades 1 to 6 ● Session 5 ● 31

Peace, Be Still Cards (Session 1)

Jesus told people about God.

Jesus and His friends got in a boat to leave.

Jesus went to sleep.

Suddenly, the wind began to blow stronger.

The waves grew bigger.

The disciples woke Jesus.

Jesus spoke to the storm.

The wind and waves obeyed Jesus.

Peace, Be Still Cards for Younger Elementary (Session 1)

Peace, Be Still Cards for Older Elementary (Session 1)

 Mark 4:33	 Mark 4:36
 Mark 4:38a	 Mark 4:37
 Mark 4:37	 Mark 4:38b
 Mark 4:39a	 Mark 4:39b

Eagle Egg Cards (Session 1)

Story Answer Cards (Session 2)

They wanted to rest.

Five loaves of bread and two fish

Over 5,000

Gave thanks to God and broke bread and fish into pieces

He healed sick people. He taught them the truth about God.

All of them

Jesus told them to because the people were hungry.

Twelve

Beaver Log Cards (Session 2)

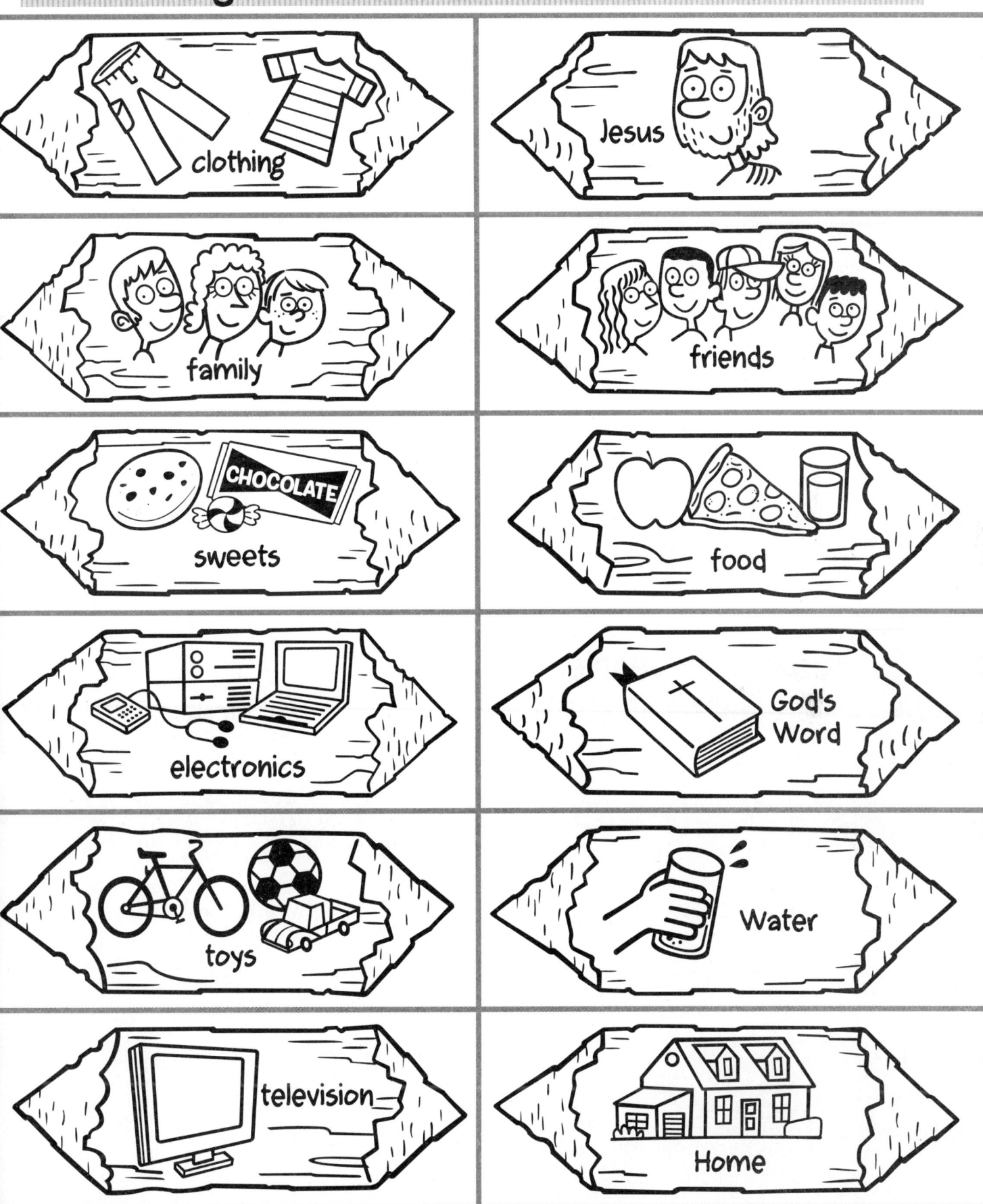

clothing	Jesus
family	friends
sweets	food
electronics	God's Word
toys	Water
television	Home

Reproducible Pages • 37

Beaver Log Cards, continued (Session 2)

My God	Christ Jesus.
will meet all	Philippians 4:19
your needs	Try Again!
according to	Try Again!
his glorious	Try Again!
riches in	Try Again!

True or False Cards for Younger Elementary (Session 2)

More than 5,000 people came to hear Jesus teach.

Nobody offered to share their food.

Jesus told the people about God.

The boy's lunch was five sandwiches and two apples.

Jesus told the disciples to give the people food.

Before feeding all the people, Jesus gave thanks to God.

The disciples went to the market to buy food.

There was no food left over.

Rock and Roll Cards (Session 3)

Crab walk to your leader.	Spin around 5 times fast.	Crawl around the circle once.	Hop on one foot 10 times.
Do 10 jumping jacks.	Pat your head and rub your tummy while counting to 10.	Give a high five to 3 friends.	Spin the bottle again!

40 ● Reproducible Pages

Rock and Roll Questions (Session 3)

Bible Story Review Questions

- **How many days was Jesus in the desert?** (Forty.)

- **What did Jesus do in the desert?** (Fasted. Prayed.)

- **Why did Satan try to get Jesus to do something wrong?** (Satan didn't want Jesus to follow God's plan. Satan didn't want Jesus to be able to take the punishment for our sins.)

- **What did Satan tempt Jesus to do with rocks?** (Turn rocks into bread.)

- **What did Satan tempt Jesus to do at the Temple?** (Jump off a high place so that angels would have to save Him.)

- **What did Satan say He would give Jesus if Jesus would worship him?** (All the kingdoms of the world.)

- **What did Jesus do every time Satan tempted Him to do wrong?** (Said "No." Repeated God's Word back to Satan.)

- **What could you do when you are tempted to do something wrong?** (Remember what God's Word says. Say what God's Word says! Pray, asking God for help. Say "No.")

Younger Elementary Questions

- **Jesus was in the desert for 12 days. True or False?** (False. Jesus was in the desert for 40 days.)

- **While in the desert, Jesus ate three good meals a day. True or False?** (False. While in the desert, Jesus didn't eat any food.)

- **Satan visited Jesus in the desert. True or False?** (True.)

- **Satan tempted Jesus to turn rocks into fish. True or False?** (False. Satan tempted Jesus to turn rocks into bread.)

- **Satan said shepherds would protect Jesus if He jumped off the roof of the Temple. True or False?** (False. Satan said angels would protect Jesus if He jumped off the roof of the Temple.)

- **Satan said he would give all the kingdoms in the world to Jesus if Jesus would worship him. True or False?** (True.)

- **Knowing God's Word helped Jesus when Satan tempted Him. True or False?** (True.)

- **When someone tempts us to do wrong, we should call them names. True or False?** (False. We should remember God's Word. We can ask God to help.)

Older Elementary Questions

- Imagine you have been alone in the desert for 40 days without anything to eat. How would you be feeling? If you were faced with the same three temptations as Jesus, which be the hardest to say "No" to? Why?

- What are some common temptations kids your age face? What are some things kids can do to help them say "No" to temptation?

- How could you say the words of 1 Corinthians 10:13 as a prayer when you are tempted to do something wrong?

- One day after VBS, your mom takes you and a friend on some errands. While you're in the grocery store and your mom is busy at the checkout, your friend steals a candy bar and tells you to take one, too. What do you do?

Pinecone Cards (Session 3)

God is faithful;

he will not let you be tempted

beyond what you can bear.

But when you are tempted,

he will also provide a way out.

1 Corinthians 10:13

Dog Bone Cards (Session 4)

This is	how we
know what	love is:
Jesus Christ	laid down
his life	for us.
1 John	3:16

© 2012 Gospel Light. Permission to photocopy granted to original purchaser only. *Climb Higher Bible Games*

Wolf Bone Cards for Older Elementary (Session 4)

That will	how they
no not	like it
like it	will be
took up	against them
2 John	6:3

Praise in Prison Cards (Session 5)

Praise in Prison Cards for Older Elementary (Session 5)

Acts 16:17

Acts 16:18

Acts 16:20-21

Acts 16:23

Acts 16:25

Acts 16:26

Acts 16:31

Acts 16:32

46 • Reproducible Pages

© 2012 Gospel Light. Permission to photocopy granted to original purchaser only. *Climb Higher Bible Games*

Caribou Cards (Session 5)

We wait in hope	for the Lord;
he is our help	and our shield.
In him our hearts rejoice,	for we trust
in his holy name.	Psalm 33:20-21

Caribou Cards for Older Elementary (Session 5)

Your best friend was beaten up by a bully while walking home from school. What can you say to help your friend?	You just tried out for the team and you didn't play well. You know you can play better than that. How can you have hope about your future now? What is still true?
Your friend has to move away and is really scared about it. What is one positive thing you could say to your friend?	Your sister told everyone a secret her friend told her. All of her friends are mad at her now. What can you say? What can you do?
You overhear your big brother lie to your mom, blaming you for something wrong that he did! Mom is mad and says you are SO grounded. What can you do? What is a good way to do that?	A good friend broke your favorite game and didn't even apologize. Now you are inviting people to your birthday party. Do you invite your friend or not? Why?

48 • Reproducible Pages © 2012 Gospel Light. Permission to photocopy granted to original purchaser only. *Climb Higher Bible Games*